T0348146

bcos
brain behaviour analysis

EXAMINER'S BOOKLET
(Version 4.3)

- 📄 *Materials required*
- ✏️ *General instructions*
- 🕐 *Time limitation*
- 👄 *Adaptation in case of aphasia*

Cognition Matters
Caring for the mind after brain injury

Contents

1A. ORIENTATION – PERSONAL INFORMATION

✎ *"I will ask you some questions."*

🕐 - *Allow a MAXIMUM of 15 sec. per question.*
- *STOP if an ERROR or NO-RESPONSE is made on all the first 3 questions.*

✏ - *In case of an unreliable verbal production, ask the examinee to write down their answers.*

1. What is your first name?	
2. What is your surname?	
3. How old are you?	
4. When were you born (day, month, year)?	
5. What is the number and name of your street?	
6. Are you left or right handed?	❏ Left　　　❏ Right　　　　❏ Ambidextrous
7. What is/was your occupation?	
8. What is your highest qualification?	❏ Primary school　　❏ Non-university diploma ❏ Secondary school　❏ University diploma ❏ College
Determine how many years the examinee has spent in education/training:	years

Condition of testing (1=normal; NT or stopped due to 2=aphasia; 3=visual/spatial; 4=confusion; 5=fatigue; 6=motor; 7=other.....)	_____
Number of correct/plausible responses NOTE: If stopped because of errors on first 3 questions, score=0/8.	_____/8
Modality of response	❏ oral ❏ written
Ask the examinee to write his/her first name with the left and the right hand and record what you judge to be the best hand here for further testing:	❏ Left　❏ Right
How well did the examinee understand the questions? (1=poor understanding even after the questions were repeated, 2=relatively good understanding but often the questions had to be repeated, 3=good understanding, almost no need to repeat the questions) NOTE: This assessment should be based on the examinee's verbal or nonverbal request(s) for repetition.	

1B. ORIENTATION – TIME AND SPACE

📄 *Test Book pp. 1–6. See www.cognitionmatters.org.uk for alternative locations options.*

✎ *"I will ask you some more questions."*
- *In the case of an ERROR or NO-RESPONSE, allow the examinee to select from the multiple choices.*

🕐 - *Allow a MAXIMUM of 15 sec. per question.*
- *STOP if an ERROR or NO-RESPONSE is given on all of the first 3 MULTIPLE CHOICE questions.*

✏ - *In case of an unreliable verbal production, give the multiple-choice questions immediately.*

	Free response	Multiple choice response			
1. Where are you right now?		❏ Church	❏ Hospital	❏ School	❏ Supermarket
2. In which city?		❏ Birmingham	❏ Manchester	❏ London	❏ Liverpool
3. What time of the day is it now?		❏ Morning	❏ Afternoon	❏ Evening	❏ Night
4. What month is it?		❏ January ❏ February ❏ March	❏ April ❏ May ❏ June	❏ July ❏ August ❏ September	❏ October ❏ November ❏ December
5. What day of the week is it?		❏ Monday ❏ Tuesday	❏ Wednesday ❏ Thursday	❏ Friday ❏ Saturday	❏ Sunday
6. What year is it?		❏ 1986	❏ 2013	❏ 2012	❏ 2011

FREE responses ONLY (condition of testing) (1=normal; NT or stopped due to 2=aphasia; 3=visual/spatial; 4=confusion; 5=fatigue; 6=motor; 7=other.....)	_____
FREE responses ONLY (number of correct responses) NOTE: If stopped because of errors and/or no-responses on the first 3 questions, score=0/6. NOTE: If skipped because of aphasia, score=NA.	_____/6
MULTIPLE CHOICE ONLY (condition of testing) (1=normal; NT/stopped due to 2=aphasia; 3=visuospatial; 4=confusion; 5=fatigue; 6=motor; 7=other: ......) NOTE: If the examinee made no errors in the free response condition, write "1".	_____
FREE responses + MULTIPLE CHOICE responses (number of correct responses) (number correct free responses + number correct multiple choice responses) NOTE: If stopped because errors and/or no-responses on first 3 questions, score=0/6.	_____/6
How well did the examinee understand the questions? (1=poor understanding even after the questions were repeated, 2=relatively good understanding but often the questions had to be repeated, 3=good understanding, almost no need to repeat the questions) NOTE: This assessment should be based on the examinee's verbal or nonverbal request(s) for repetition.	

1C. ORIENTATION – NOSOGNOSIA

✏️ **"I have still a few questions."**

🕐 *- Allow a MAXIMUM of 15 sec. per question.*

1. Why are/were you in hospital?	
2a. Can you show me your right hand? 2b. Can you show me your left hand?	
3. Do you have any problems moving your arms or legs?	

Condition of testing (1=normal; NT or stopped due to 2=aphasia; 3=visual/spatial; 4=confusion; 5=fatigue; 6=motor; 7=other.....)	_____
Number of correct responses	_____ /3

How well did the examinee understand the questions? (1=poor understanding even after the questions were repeated, 2=relatively good understanding but often the questions had to be repeated, 3=good understanding, almost no need to repeat the questions) NOTE: This assessment should be based on the examinee's verbal or nonverbal request(s) for repetition.	

2. PICTURE NAMING

📄 *Test Book pp. 7–20.*

✏️ **"I will show you some pictures and ask you for the name of each object."**

🕐 *- Allow a MAXIMUM of 15 sec. per picture.*
- STOP if there are ERRORS or NO-RESPONSE for any of the first 4 pictures.

	Response
1. Bell	
2. Peas	
3. Grapes	
4. Umbrella	
5. Raspberry	
6. Colander	
7. Leek	
8. Stopwatch	
9. Bat	
10. Pineapple	
11. Chisel	
12. Tiger	
13. Hook	
14. Spanner	

Condition of testing (1=normal; NT or stopped due to 2=aphasia; 3=visual/spatial; 4=confusion; 5=fatigue; 6=motor; 7=other.....)	_____
Number of correct responses NOTE: If stopped because of errors and/or no-responses to the first 4 pictures, score=0/14.	_____ /14

NOTES:
1) Plural and singular forms are equally acceptable.
2) Synonyms such as "strainer" and "colander" are equally acceptable.
3) "Blackberry" is an acceptable response for the picture of a raspberry.
4) Visually similar items such as "clock" or "pocket clock" for "stopwatch" or "spring onions" for "leek" CANNOT be accepted as correct responses.
5) Phonological/phonemic distortions should be considered as errors.

3. SENTENCE CONSTRUCTION

📄 *Test Book pp. 21–25. See Appendix 4 of the Manual for scoring examples.*

✏️ **"I will show you a photograph and give you two words. Can you please tell me what the person is doing? Use only one sentence and include the two words. The sentence should fit with what you see in the photograph. For example, if I show you this picture** (show the first picture) **and these two words 'sugar' and 'tea', you could make a sentence such as: The man is putting some sugar in his tea."**
- *For each picture, GIVE the prompt as indicated below AND read aloud the written pair of words.*
- *If the examinee describes the photograph in more than one sentence, instruct the examinee to rephrase using one sentence. Rephrasing is only allowed once per trial.*

🕐 - *Allow a MAXIMUM of 30 sec. per picture.*
- *STOP if NO-RESPONSE is given to the first picture.*

Prompt	Response
1. Describe what the person is doing in one sentence and use the words "Book – bag".	

If the examinee uses an active sentence:
(e.g., the woman is putting the book in her bag)
❏ *Correct use of subject ("she" or "the woman" or "a woman")*
❏ *Correct use of verb ("puts" or "is putting" or "takes" or "is taking")*
❏ *Correct use of direct object ("the book" or "her book" or "a book")*
❏ *Correct use of adverb phrase (is putting…"in the bag" or is putting… "in her bag" or is taking "from the bag" or is taking "from the bag")*
NOTE1: synonyms can be accepted
NOTE2: the passive sentence is not accepted in response to the prompt

| 2. Describe what the person is doing in one sentence and use the words "Coat – man". | |

If the examinee uses an active sentence with the verb "help":
(e.g., the man is helping the woman (to) put her coat on)
❏ *Correct use of subject ("the man" or "a man")*
❏ *Correct use of verb ("helps…(to) put(…)on" or "is helping…(to) put(…)on" or "helps with" or "is helping with")*
❏ *Correct use of direct object 1 ("the woman" or "her")*
❏ *Correct use of direct object 2 ("her coat" or "the woman's coat")*

If the examinee uses an active sentence without the verb "help":
(e.g., the man is putting the coat on the woman)
❏ *Correct use of subject ("the man" or "a man")*
❏ *Correct use of verb ("is putting(…)on" or "puts(…)on")*
❏ *Correct use of direct object ("coat")*
❏ *Correct use of adverb phrase ("on the woman")*

If the examinee uses a passive sentence with the verb "help":
(e.g., the woman is being helped by the man to put her coat on)
❏ *Correct use of subject ("she" or "the woman" or " a woman")*
❏ *Correct use of verb ("is being helped (to) put(…)on" or "is helped (to) put(…)on")*
❏ *Correct use of agent ("by the man" or "by a man")*
❏ *Correct use of direct object with possessive ("her coat")*

If the examinee uses a passive sentence without the verb "help":
(e.g., the woman is having her coat put on by the man)
❏ *Correct use of subject ("she" or "the woman" or "a man")*
❏ *Correct use of verb ("is having… put(…)on")*
❏ *Correct use of agent ("by the man" or "by a man")*
❏ *Correct use of direct object with possessive ("her coat")*
NOTE: synonyms can be accepted

Condition of testing (1=normal; NT or stopped due to 2=aphasia; 3=visual/spatial; 4=confusion; 5=fatigue; 6=motor; 7=other.....)	
Total number of correct responses NOTE: If stopped because no-response has been made for the first picture, score=0/8.	/8
How well did the examinee understand the instructions? (1=poor understanding even after the instructions were repeated, 2=relatively good understanding but the instructions had to be repeated, 3=good understanding, no need to repeat the instructions) NOTE: This assessment should be based on the examinee's verbal or nonverbal request(s) for repetition.	

4. SENTENCE READING

📄 *Test Book pp. 26–27, stopwatch.*

✏️ *- Hide the sentences while giving the instructions.*
   "Now, I will show you a page with a sentence. Please read the sentence aloud as quickly and as accurately as possible. You can start when I say GO."
   - Once the page is placed in front of the examinee, say "go" and record the time taken to read the sentence.
   - Stop timing when the examinee finishes the pronunciation of the last item on the page.

🕐 *- STOP if NO-RESPONSE is made to the first sentence.*

Response
The <u>swords</u> and <u>treasures</u>,
which belong to the <u>viscount</u>,
are kept in his <u>castle</u>.

Time: **sec.**

After we <u>listened</u> to the award-winning concert at our <u>daughter'</u>s house, we took a <u>leisurely</u> walk home while debating whether the jury members had been impartial.

Time: **sec.**

Condition of testing	_____
(1=normal; NT or stopped due to 2=aphasia; 3=visual/spatial; 4=confusion; 5=fatigue; 6=motor; 7=other.....)	
Total time	_____ sec.
(summing the time for both the sentences) NOTE: If stopped because no-response to the first sentence, score=NA.	
Total number of words correctly read	_____ /42
(subtract 1 point for each word addition) NOTE: If stopped because no-response has been made for the first sentence, score=0/42.	

NOTES:
1) Exception words are underlined.
2) Auto-corrections are accepted.
3) Phonological/phonemic distortions should be considered as errors.

5. NONWORD READING

📄 *Test Book pp. 28–29, stopwatch.*

✏️ **"Now I will show you a page with 3 written nonwords, that is, words that do not exist. Please read them aloud as quickly and as accurately as possible. You can start when I say GO."**
   - Once the nonwords are visible to the examinee, say "go" and record the time taken to read the words.
   - Stop timing when the examinee finishes the pronunciation of the last item on the page.
   - Repeat the instructions for each test page.

🕐 *- STOP if NO-RESPONSE is made to the first 3 nonwords.*

	Response			
1. dwend (with **en** like in *end*)		**Number correct responses:**		/3
2. brilt (with **i** like in *bill*)		**Total time:**		sec.
3. flosp (with **o** like in *pot*)				
4. glurms (with **ur** like in *urn*)		**Number correct responses:**		/3
5. shreel (with **ee** like in *wheel*)		**Total time:**		sec.
6. vench (with **en** like in *bench*)				

Condition of testing	_____
(1=normal; NT or stopped due to 2=aphasia; 3=visual/spatial; 4=confusion; 5=fatigue; 6=motor; 7=other.....)	
Total time	_____ sec.
(summing the time for the 2 sets of nonwords) NOTE: If stopped because no-response has been made for the first 3 words, score=NA.	
Number of correct responses	_____ /6
NOTE: If stopped because no-response was made to the first 3 words, score=0/6.	

6. STORY RECALL AND RECOGNITION – IMMEDIATE RECALL

📄   *Test Book pp. 30–44, stopwatch.*

✏️   ***"I will read you a story. Listen carefully because I will ask you to recall as many details of the story as possible afterwards."*** *Make sure the examinee is listening to you before starting to read the story.*
- *Read the story only ONCE. Then ask for free recall of the story.*
- *At the END of the free recall, present the corresponding multiple choice trials for any items that were either not reported, reported incompletely or reported incorrectly.*
- *Give FEEDBACK on the multiple choice questions.*

🕐   *- Allow a MAXIMUM of 2 min. for the FREE recall.*
- *If no response after 30 sec., give non-specific prompts (e.g., "how did the story start?") every 30 sec.*
- *Allow a MAXIMUM of 15 sec. for each set of MULTIPLE choices.*
- *If ERRORS and/or NO-RESPONSES occur on ALL 5 first questions, GIVE the responses for questions 6 to 12 IMMEDIATELY, and ask again for a response to question 13.*

👄   *- If no reliable verbal response can be produced, give the multiple choice possibilities.*

Mrs Davis / from Manchester / met her neighbour / in the supermarket /. She told her that she had been robbed / the day before / while coming out of the post office /, just after having drawn her pension /. The two thieves /, who were teenage boys /, managed to get twenty-five pounds / from her handbag /. A passer-by who was a trainee police officer /, caught the thieves / just round the corner /.

Segments	Free recall 1		Recognition 1 (for error or omissions only)	
1) Mrs Davis	*(1)* ❑ *Mrs Davis*	*(0.5)* ❑ *Lady or Mr Davis*	1) What is the name of the person in the story? 1 **2** 3 4	*(1)* ❑ *correct in free recall* *(1)* ❑ *correct in MC*
2) Manchester	*(1)* ❑ *Manchester*		2) Where is she from? 1 2 **3** 4	*(1)* ❑ *correct in free recall* *(1)* ❑ *correct in MC*
3) Neighbour	*(1)* ❑ *Neighbour*		3) Who did she meet? 1 **2** 3 4	*(1)* ❑ *correct in free recall* *(1)* ❑ *correct in MC*
4) Supermarket	*(1)* ❑ *Supermarket*	*(0.5)* ❑ *Shop*	4) Where did she meet her? 1 2 3 **4**	*(1)* ❑ *correct in free recall* *(1)* ❑ *correct in MC*
5) Had been robbed	*(1)* ❑ *Robbed*	*(0.5)* ❑ *Attacked*	5) What did she tell her? 1 **2** 3 4	*(1)* ❑ *correct in free recall* *(1)* ❑ *correct in MC*
6) The day before	*(1)* ❑ *Day before*		6) When was she robbed? **1** 2 3 4	*(1)* ❑ *correct in free recall* *(1)* ❑ *correct in MC*
7) Post office	*(1)* ❑ *Coming out of post office*	*(0.5)* ❑ *(in) Post office*	7) Where was she robbed? 1 2 3 **4**	*(1)* ❑ *correct in free recall* *(1)* ❑ *correct in MC*
8) Pension	*(1)* ❑ *Drew her pension*	*(0.5)* ❑ *(was going to draw) Pension*	8) What was she doing at the post office? 1 2 **3** 4	*(1)* ❑ *correct in free recall* *(1)* ❑ *correct in MC*
9) Two	*(1)* ❑ *Two*		9) How many thieves were there? 1 2 3 **4**	*(1)* ❑ *correct in free recall* *(1)* ❑ *correct in MC*
10) Teenage boys	*(1)* ❑ *Teenage boys*	*(0.5)* ❑ *Boys*	10) Who were the thieves? 1 2 3 **4**	*(1)* ❑ *correct in free recall* *(1)* ❑ *correct in MC*
11) 25 pounds	*(1)* ❑ *25 pounds*		11) How much did they steal? 1 2 **3** 4	*(1)* ❑ *correct in free recall* *(1)* ❑ *correct in MC*
12) Handbag	*(1)* ❑ *Handbag*	*(0.5)* ❑ *Bag*	12) Where did they steal the money from? 1 2 **3** 4	*(1)* ❑ *correct in free recall* *(1)* ❑ *correct in MC*
13) Caught	*(1)* ❑ *Were caught*		13) What happened to the thieves at the end? **1** 2 3 4	*(1)* ❑ *correct in free recall* *(1)* ❑ *correct in MC*
14) Trainee police officer	*(1)* ❑ *Trainee police officer*	*(0.5)* ❑ *Police*	14) Who caught the thieves? 1 **2** 3 4	*(1)* ❑ *correct in free recall* *(1)* ❑ *correct in MC*
15) Round the corner	*(1)* ❑ *Round the corner*		15) Where were the thieves caught? **1** 2 3 4	*(1)* ❑ *correct in free recall* *(1)* ❑ *correct in MC*

FREE recall ONLY – condition of testing (1=normal; NT or stopped due to 2=aphasia; 3=visual/spatial; 4=confusion; 5=fatigue; 6=motor; 7=other.....)	_____
FREE recall ONLY – total score (summing the "1" and "0.5" points columns)	_____/15
RECOGNITION ONLY – condition of testing (1=normal; NT or stopped due to 2=aphasia; 3=visual/spatial; 4=confusion; 5=fatigue; 6=motor; 7=other.....)	_____
FREE recall + RECOGNITION total score (summing the "1" points column BUT NOT the "0.5" points column) NOTE: If you skipped trials 6 to 12 in the multiple choice, give 0 points for trials 6 to 12.	_____/15

NOTE: Synonyms can be scored as "1"; information that is partially complete should be scored as "0.5".

Comments (confabulations, perseverations etc.):

6

7. APPLE CANCELLATION

📄   *Examinee's Booklet and stopwatch.*

✎   **"I will show you a page with apples. Sometimes, the apple is complete, sometimes incomplete. Please cross out the complete apples only. Try this example first."** *Give the example and correct if necessary. Two practice trials can be presented (but not more).*
"I give you a few minutes to do the same on this page. Please don't move the page." *Place the test sheet in a landscape position with the black triangle nearest to the examinee's midline and start recording the time.*
- Do NOT give any cues for the test sheet.

🕐   *- STOP if NO-RESPONSE is made on the practice sheet.*
- Allow a MAXIMUM of 5 min. for the task.

Scoring transparancy can be found in the Test Book.

Boxes as indicated on the template below:

Box1		Box3		Box5		Box7		Box9	
No. correct:	/5	No. correct:	/5	No. correct:	/5	No. correct:	/5	No. correct:	/5
No. false positives		No. false positives		No. false positives		No. false positives		No. false positives	
with Right opening:	/5	with Right opening:	/5	with Right opening:	/5	with Right opening:	/5	with Right opening:	/5
with Left opening:	/5	with Left opening:	/5	with Left opening:	/5	with Left opening:	/5	with Left opening:	/5
Box2		**Box4**		**Box6**		**Box8**		**Box10**	
No. correct:	/5	No. correct:	/5	No. correct:	/5	No. correct:	/5	No. correct:	/5
No. false positives		No. false positives		No. false positives		No. false positives		No. false positives	
with Right opening:	/5	with Right opening:	/5	with Right opening:	/5	with Right opening:	/5	with Right opening:	/5
with Left opening:	/5	with Left opening:	/5	with Left opening:	/5	with Left opening:	/5	with Left opening:	/5

Condition of testing (1=normal; NT or stopped due to 2=aphasia; 3=visual/spatial; 4=confusion; 5=fatigue; 6=motor; 7=other.....)	_____
Total number of complete apples selected	_____ /50
Total number of false positives with RIGHT opening	_____ /50
Total number of false positives with LEFT opening	_____ /50
Asymmetry score for the complete apple (no. correct in boxes 7 + 8 + 9 + 10) *minus* (no. correct in boxes 1 + 2 + 3 + 4)	_____
Asymmetry score for the incomplete apple (no. false positives with LEFT opening) minus (no. false positives with RIGHT opening)	_____

Template for scoring the Apple cancellation test (re-scaled):

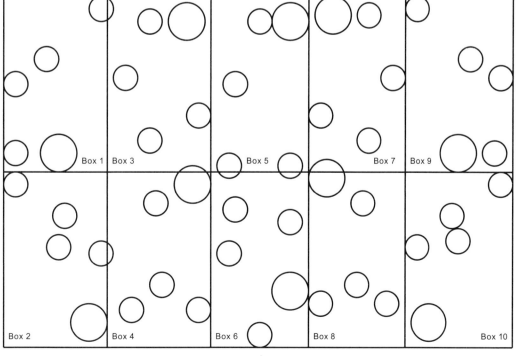

Apple Cancellation Task Scoring Transparency

8. VISUAL EXTINCTION

> ✏️   *- Place yourself approximately 1 metre opposite the examinee and at their midline.*
> *- Hold up the index finger of your left and right hand on either side of your head (approximately 20 cm from your nose). Say:*
> **"Look at my nose. Don't move your eyes. I will move my finger either on your left, on your right or on both sides simultaneously. Please tell me or show me by pointing which side moved. Always keep looking at my nose."**
> *- For each trial, bend your finger(s) twice.*
>
> 🕐   *- Allow a MAXIMUM of 15 sec. per trial.*
> *- STOP if NO-RESPONSE is made on the first 3 trials.*

(R=right; L=left; B=bilateral):

Hands to use from your perspective	Examinee's response	Examinee's perspective (expected responses)
R B L		L B R
B B R		B B L
B L L		B R R
B B L		B B R
R B		L B
R B		L B

Condition of testing	_____
(1=normal; NT or stopped due to 2=aphasia; 3=visual/spatial; 4=confusion; 5=fatigue; 6=motor; 7=other.....)	
LEFT UNILATERAL – number of correct detections NOTE: If stopped because no-response has been made for the first 3 items, score=0.	_____ /4
RIGHT UNILATERAL – number of correct detections NOTE: If stopped because no-response has been made for the first 3 items, score=0.	_____ /4
LEFT BILATERAL – number of correct detections NOTE: If stopped because no-response has been made for the first 3 items, score=0.	_____ /8
RIGHT BILATERAL – number of correct detections NOTE: If stopped because no-response has been made for the first 3 items, score=0.	_____ /8
NOTE: If the examinee perceives unilateral stimuli to be bilateral, mark as an error.	

9. TACTILE EXTINCTION

✎   - *Place yourself opposite the examinee and at their midline. Say:*
   "Put your hands on your knees (or on the bed cover). Now, close your eyes. I will touch your hand, either your left hand, your right hand or both your hands simultaneously. Please tell me or show me by lifting your hand briefly which hand I touched. Always keep your eyes closed."
   - *Make sure the examinee is sitting or lying straight and symmetrically (no crossed arms or legs).*
   - *For each trial, touch by gently tapping twice with your hand the dorsal part of the examinee's hand.*

🕐   - *Allow a MAXIMUM of 15 sec. per trial.*
   - *STOP if NO-RESPONSE is made for the first 3 trials.*

(R=right; L=left; B=bilateral):

Hands to use from your perspective	Examinee's response	Examinee's perspective (expected responses)
B B L		B B R
B L B		B R B
B R R		B L L
B B R		B B L
B L		B R
R L		L R

Condition of testing (1=normal; NT or stopped due to 2=aphasia; 3=visual/spatial; 4=confusion; 5=fatigue; 6=motor; 7=other.....)	_____
LEFT UNILATERAL – number of correct detections NOTE: If stopped because no-response has been made for the first 3 items, score=0.	_____ /4
RIGHT UNILATERAL – number of correct detections NOTE: If stopped because no-response has been made for the first 3 items, score=0.	_____ /4
LEFT BILATERAL – number of correct detections NOTE: If stopped because no-response has been made for the first 3 items, score=0.	_____ /8
RIGHT BILATERAL – number of correct detections NOTE: If stopped because no-response has been made for the first 3 items, score=0.	_____ /8
NOTE: If the examinee perceives unilateral stimuli to be bilateral, mark as an error.	

10. RULE FINDING AND CONCEPT SWITCHING TEST

📄 *Test Book pp. 45–68.*

✏️ ***"You will see a grid with a black dot. Can you please point to the black dot?"*** *Show where the black dot is if the examinee cannot point to it. Then ask the examinee again to point to the black dot (this is just to ensure that they can give a reliable pointing response). Stop the task if the examinee cannot point reliably on the second attempt.*
"Ok. This dot will now move from page to page to a specific location. It can move to any of the grey or the coloured squares. The dot does not move randomly but follows a pattern. However, the rule governing the pattern can change. Look carefully at how the dot moves on each trial. You have to anticipate and show me where the dot will move next. Please remain attentive so that you can keep track of the changes."
- Present the practice trials saying:
"So for instance, if the dot is first here, then moves here *(show the second practice trial),* ***where is the dot most likely to move next?*** *(show the third practice trial)"*
- Correct the examinee's response on the third practice item if necessary.
- When showing the trials, ALWAYS keep the previous trial directly above for the examinee to see.
- When showing the trials, point to the black dot.
- If the examinee does not know the location of the dot, ask him/her to guess.

🕐 *- Allow a MAXIMUM of 15 sec. per trial.*
- STOP if FEWER THAN 2 CORRECT responses are given up to TRIAL 11.

	Rule	Stimulus	Expected response	Actual response	Accuracy 0/1	
1	To the right	B3	any		■	
2	To the right	C3	D3			
3	To the right	D3	E3			
4	To the right	E3	F3			Cross dimension switch
5	To red	B5	E3			
6	To red	E3	B5			
7	To red	B5	E3			
8	To red	E3	B5			
9	To red	B5	E3			
10	To red	E3	B5			
11	To red	B5	E3			Within dimension switch
12	To red	E6	B5			
13	To green	B5	E6			
14	To red	E6	B5			
15	To green	B5	E6			
16	To red	E6	B5			
17	To green	B5	E6			
18	To red	E6	B5			
19	To green	B5	E6			

Condition of testing (1=normal; NT or stopped due to 2=aphasia; 3=visual/spatial; 4=confusion; 5=fatigue; 6=motor; 7=other.....)	_____
Pointing PRETEST score (2=points correctly on the first attempt; 1=points correctly on the second attempt; 0=cannot point reliably)	_____
Number of correct responses NOTE: If stopped because no-response has been made up to trial 11, score=number correct until trial 11 /18.	_____ /18
Number of correct rules detected (number of rules that are applied correctly on at least 2 consecutive trials) NOTE: If stopped because no-response has been made up to trial 11, score=number correct rules until trial 11 /3.	_____ /3
How well did the examinee understand the instructions? (1=poor understanding even after the instructions were repeated, 2=relatively good understanding but the instructions had to be repeated, 3=good understanding, no need to repeat the instructions) NOTE: This assessment should be based on the performance on the practice trials and the examinee's verbal or nonverbal request(s) for repetition.	

11. AUDITORY ATTENTION

📖   *CD, Test Book pp. 69–72 for aphasic examinees. (Audio stimuli also available from www.cognitionmatters.org.uk)*

✎   ***"You will hear a recording with a man saying different words. When the man says 'hello', 'please' or 'no' you have to tap on the table. When the man says something else, just ignore him. So the three words you have to respond to are: hello, please and no. Can you repeat these words?"*** *(if the examinee does not recall the three words, repeat the words).* ***"We will start with an example."***
- *Where indicated on the protocol below, ask the examinee to recall the three target words.*
- *Practice should be repeated until the examinee makes no errors in a practice block OR can correctly recall the three target words after the practice block. If after the third practice block these conditions are not met, continue the test ONLY if the examinee tapped (correctly or incorrectly) to at least one of the spoken items.*

🕐   - *STOP if MORE THAN 8 ERRORS have occurred at the end of ANY BLOCK (block 1 OR block 2) but DO NOT FORGET to ASK for the three correct words at the end.*

👂   *When asking for the target words, present a multiple choice.*

PRACTICE 1
"Can you tell me the three words you have to respond to?"_____

1. Please	❏ **Taps**	❏ Does not tap
2. Thanks	❏ Taps	❏ **Does not tap**
3. Goodbye	❏ Taps	❏ **Does not tap**
4. Hello	❏ **Taps**	❏ Does not tap
5. Yes	❏ Taps	❏ **Does not tap**
6. No	❏ **Taps**	❏ Does not tap

"Can you tell me the three words you have to respond to?"_____

PRACTICE 2 (if necessary)
"Can you tell me the three words you have to respond to?"_____

1. Please	❏ **Taps**	❏ Does not tap
2. Thanks	❏ Taps	❏ **Does not tap**
3. Goodbye	❏ Taps	❏ **Does not tap**
4. Hello	❏ **Taps**	❏ Does not tap
5. Yes	❏ Taps	❏ **Does not tap**
6. No	❏ **Taps**	❏ Does not tap

"Can you tell me the three words you have to respond to?"_____

PRACTICE 3 (if necessary)
"Can you tell me the three words you have to respond to?"_____

1. Please	❏ **Taps**	❏ Does not tap
2. Thanks	❏ Taps	❏ **Does not tap**
3. Goodbye	❏ Taps	❏ **Does not tap**
4. Hello	❏ **Taps**	❏ Does not tap
5. Yes	❏ Taps	❏ **Does not tap**
6. No	❏ **Taps**	❏ Does not tap

"Can you tell me the three words you have to respond to?"_____

TEST
Block 1

Hello	❏ **Taps**	❏ Does not tap
Thanks	❏ Taps	❏ **Does not tap**
Goodbye	❏ Taps	❏ **Does not tap**
Yes	❏ Taps	❏ **Does not tap**
Please	❏ **Taps**	❏ Does not tap
No	❏ **Taps**	❏ Does not tap
Yes	❏ Taps	❏ **Does not tap**
Thanks	❏ Taps	❏ **Does not tap**
No	❏ **Taps**	❏ Does not tap
Hello	❏ **Taps**	❏ Does not tap
Goodbye	❏ Taps	❏ **Does not tap**
Please	❏ **Taps**	❏ Does not tap
Yes	❏ Taps	❏ **Does not tap**
Please	❏ **Taps**	❏ Does not tap
Thanks	❏ Taps	❏ **Does not tap**
Goodbye	❏ Taps	❏ **Does not tap**
Hello	❏ **Taps**	❏ Does not tap
No	❏ **Taps**	❏ Does not tap

Block 2

Hello	❑ **Taps**	❑ Does not tap
No	❑ **Taps**	❑ Does not tap
Yes	❑ Taps	❑ **Does not tap**
Please	❑ **Taps**	❑ Does not tap
Goodbye	❑ Taps	❑ **Does not tap**
No	❑ **Taps**	❑ Does not tap
Goodbye	❑ Taps	❑ **Does not tap**
Please	❑ **Taps**	❑ Does not tap
Yes	❑ Taps	❑ **Does not tap**
Hello	❑ **Taps**	❑ Does not tap
Thanks	❑ Taps	❑ **Does not tap**
Goodbye	❑ Taps	❑ **Does not tap**
No	❑ **Taps**	❑ Does not tap
Hello	❑ **Taps**	❑ Does not tap
Thanks	❑ Taps	❑ **Does not tap**
Yes	❑ Taps	❑ **Does not tap**
Thanks	❑ Taps	❑ **Does not tap**
Please	❑ **Taps**	❑ Does not tap

Block 3

Yes	❑ Taps	❑ **Does not tap**
Please	❑ **Taps**	❑ Does not tap
Yes	❑ Taps	❑ **Does not tap**
No	❑ **Taps**	❑ Does not tap
Please	❑ **Taps**	❑ Does not tap
Goodbye	❑ Taps	❑ **Does not tap**
Thanks	❑ Taps	❑ **Does not tap**
Goodbye	❑ Taps	❑ **Does not tap**
No	❑ **Taps**	❑ Does not tap
Thanks	❑ Taps	❑ **Does not tap**
Hello	❑ **Taps**	❑ Does not tap
Please	❑ **Taps**	❑ Does not tap
Thanks	❑ Taps	❑ **Does not tap**
No	❑ **Taps**	❑ Does not tap
Hello	❑ **Taps**	❑ Does not tap
Yes	❑ Taps	❑ **Does not tap**
Goodbye	❑ Taps	❑ **Does not tap**
Hello	❑ **Taps**	❑ Does not tap

Can you tell me the three words you had to respond to? _____

	Block 1	Block 2	Block 3
Number of correct responses:	/18	/18	/18
Number of false positives:	/9	/9	/9
Number of omissions:	/9	/9	/9

Condition of testing (1=normal; NT or stopped due to 2=aphasia; 3=visual/spatial; 4=confusion; 5=fatigue; 6=motor; 7=other......)	_____
Total number of correct responses NOTE: If you stopped after block 1 or 2, score=total number of correct responses until you stopped /54	_____/54
Total number of false positives NOTE: If you stopped after block 1 or 2, score= total number of false positives until you stopped.	_____/27
Total number of omissions NOTE: If you stopped after block 1 or 2, score= total number of omissions until you stopped.	_____/27
Sustained attention index (number of correct responses in block 1 minus number of correct responses in block 3) NOTE: If you stopped after block 1 or 2, score=NA.	_____
Response mode for recalling the target words	❑ free response ❑ multiple choice
Number of practices required	_____/3
Number of words recalled at the end of the test	_____/3
How well did the examinee understand the instructions? (1=poor understanding even after the instructions were repeated, 2=relatively good understanding but the instructions had to be repeated, 3=good understanding, no need to repeat the instructions) NOTE: This assessment should be based on the performance on the practice trials and the examinee's verbal or nonverbal request(s) for repetition.	

12. STORY RECALL AND RECOGNITION – DELAYED RECALL

📄   *Test Book pp. 73–87, stopwatch.*

✏️   ***"I read a story to you earlier on. Can you now tell me all the details of the story you remember?"***
- Do NOT read the story.
- At the END of the free recall, present the corresponding multiple choice trials for any items that were either not reported, reported incompletely or reported incorrectly.
- FEEDBACK is NOT necessary.

🕐   - Allow a MAXIMUM of 2 min. for the FREE recall.
- If no response after 30 sec., give non-specific prompts (e.g., "how did the story start?") every 30 sec.
- Allow a MAXIMUM of 15 sec. For each MULTIPLE choice recognition test.
- If ERRORS and/or NO-RESPONSES on <u>ALL</u> the first 5 questions, give the responses for questions 6 to 12 IMMEDIATELY, and ask for a response for question 13 again.

👄   *If no reliable verbal response can be produced, give the multiple choice possibilities.*

Segments	Free recall 1		Recognition 1 (for error or omissions only)	
1) Mrs Davis	*(1)* ☐ *Mrs Davis*	*(0.5)* ☐ *Lady or Mr Davis*	1) What is the name of the person in the story? 1 2 3 **4**	*(1)* ☐ *correct in free recall* *(1)* ☐ *correct in MC*
2) Manchester	*(1)* ☐ *Manchester*		2) Where is she from? **1** 2 3 4	*(1)* ☐ *correct in free recall* *(1)* ☐ *correct in MC*
3) Neighbour	*(1)* ☐ *Neighbour*		3) Who did she meet? 1 2 **3** 4	*(1)* ☐ *correct in free recall* *(1)* ☐ *correct in MC*
4) Supermarket	*(1)* ☐ *Supermarket*	*(0.5)* ☐ *Shop*	4) Where did she meet her? **1** 2 3 4	*(1)* ☐ *correct in free recall* *(1)* ☐ *correct in MC*
5) Had been robbed	*(1)* ☐ *Robbed*	*(0.5)* ☐ *Attacked*	5) What did she tell? 1 2 **3** 4	*(1)* ☐ *correct in free recall* *(1)* ☐ *correct in MC*
6) The day before	*(1)* ☐ *Day before*		6) When was she robbed? 1 **2** 3 4	*(1)* ☐ *correct in free recall* *(1)* ☐ *correct in MC*
7) Post office	*(1)* ☐ *Coming out of post office*	*(0.5)* ☐ *(in) Post office*	7) Where was she robbed? 1 **2** 3 4	*(1)* ☐ *correct in free recall* *(1)* ☐ *correct in MC*
8) Pension	*(1)* ☐ *Drew her pension*	*(0.5)* ☐ *(was going to draw) Pension*	8) What was she doing at the post office? **1** 2 3 4	*(1)* ☐ *correct in free recall* *(1)* ☐ *correct in MC*
9) Two	*(1)* ☐ *Two*		9) How many thieves were there? 1 **2** 3 4	*(1)* ☐ *correct in free recall* *(1)* ☐ *correct in MC*
10) Teenage boys	*(1)* ☐ *Teenage boys*	*(0.5)* ☐ *Boys or teenage thieves*	10) Who were the thieves? 1 2 **3** 4	*(1)* ☐ *correct in free recall* *(1)* ☐ *correct in MC*
11) 25 pounds	*(1)* ☐ *25 pounds*		11) How much did they steal? **1** 2 3 4	*(1)* ☐ *correct in free recall* *(1)* ☐ *correct in MC*
12) Handbag	*(1)* ☐ *Handbag*	*(0.5)* ☐ *Bag*	12) Where did they steal the money from? 1 2 3 **4**	*(1)* ☐ *correct in free recall* *(1)* ☐ *correct in MC*
13) Caught	*(1)* ☐ *Were caught*		13) What happened to the thieves at the end? 1 2 3 **4**	*(1)* ☐ *correct in free recall* *(1)* ☐ *correct in MC*
14) Trainee police officer	*(1)* ☐ *Trainee police officer*	*(0.5)* ☐ *Police*	14) Who caught the thieves? 1 2 3 **4**	*(1)* ☐ *correct in free recall* *(1)* ☐ *correct in MC*
15) Round the corner	*(1)* ☐ *Round the corner*		15) Where were the thieves caught? 1 2 **3** 4	*(1)* ☐ *correct in free recall* *(1)* ☐ *correct in MC*

FREE recall ONLY – condition of testing (1=normal; NT or stopped due to 2=aphasia; 3=visual/spatial; 4=confusion; 5=fatigue; 6=motor; 7=other.....)	_____
FREE recall ONLY – total score (summing the "1" and "0.5" points columns)	_____ /15
RECOGNITION ONLY – condition of testing (1=normal; NT or stopped due to 2=aphasia; 3=visual/spatial; 4=confusion; 5=fatigue; 6=motor; 7=other.....)	_____
FREE recall + RECOGNITION total score (summing the "1" points BUT NOT the "0.5" points columns) NOTE: if you skipped trials 6 to 12 in the multiple choice, give 0 points for trials 6 to 12.	_____ /15
NOTE: Synonyms can be scored as "1"; information that is partially complete should be scored as "0.5".	

Comments (confabulations, perseverations etc.):

13. MULTI-STEP OBJECT USE

📄   *Test Book p. 88 and objects from the zipped bag.*

✏️   *- Arrange the objects in midline, in the order of: (nearest to the examinee) matches, batteries, glue stick, screwdriver, torch (furthest from the examinee).*
     - Show the picture of the lighted torch.
     "Please can you make the torch work, everything you need is here for you. Do the best you can."
     - For examinees with unilateral weakness, the examiner can help e.g., stabilising the torch barrel on the examinee's request or when examinees show signs of initiating the appropriate action.
     - As much as possible, make sure every action step of the examinee is observed and recorded for reliable scoring.

🕐   *- If after 30 sec. the examinee fails to initiate any given step, then repeat the instruction and show the picture.*
     - STOP if the examinee still FAILS TO INITIATE any given step.

SEQUENCE	Order	Description
Open barrel		
Put batteries in		
Close barrel		
Switch torch on		
Other:		

For each criterion take into account only the examinee's FIRST attempt to complete the step.
Give 1 point for each criterion achieved on first attempt.

Start by unscrewing the barrel (after checking if torch works) WITHOUT any cue from the examiner	❏ 0 point	❏ 1 point
Fill barrel after opening	❏ 0 point	❏ 1 point
Insert batteries from the cylindrical opening	❏ 0 point	❏ 1 point
2 batteries inserted	❏ 0 point	❏ 1 point
Close barrel after inserting the batteries	❏ 0 point	❏ 1 point
Top replaced the right way and screwed in	❏ 0 point	❏ 1 point
Switch torch on after closing barrel	❏ 0 point	❏ 1 point
Maximum 2 attempts to insert the batteries the right way	❏ 0 point	❏ 1 point
Torch lit up eventually	❏ 0 point	❏ 1 point
No use of irrelevant objects	❏ 0 point	❏ 1 point
No irrelevant actions with the target objects	❏ 0 point	❏ 1 point
No perseveration	❏ 0 point	❏ 1 point

Condition of testing (1=normal; NT or stopped due to 2=aphasia; 3=visual/spatial; 4=confusion; 5=fatigue; 6=motor; 7=other.....)	_____
Hand used	❏ left only ❏ right only ❏ both hands
Total score (summing points)	_____/12

14. GESTURE PRODUCTION

📄 *Test Book pp. 89–100.*

✎ **"This is the gesture for 'be quiet'."** *Show the word and demonstrate the gesture.*
"Now, I will ask you to carry out some gestures for me. Can you please be as precise as possible. Could you show me the gesture for...with your right (or left) hand?" *Choose the examinee's best hand (refer to your record of the examinee's best hand in task 1A).*
- Show and read aloud the written name of each gesture, one at a time.
- Please follow the detailed scoring instructions below and describe the examinee's errors in the "comments" section whenever possible.

🕐 *- Allow a MAXIMUM of 15 sec. per item.*

INTRANSITIVE	Scoring**			Comments
1. Hitch-hiking	❑ 2 points	❑ 1 point	❑ 0 point	
2. Military salute	❑ 2 points	❑ 1 point	❑ 0 point	
3. Stop	❑ 2 points	❑ 1 point	❑ 0 point	
Total score:		**/6**		

** Give 0 points for (1) no response after 15 sec. or (2) an unrecognisable gesture (e.g., for *hitch-hiking*, shaking open palm forwards) or (3) a perseveration from the previous gesture.
Give 1 point for a recognisable but inaccurate gesture: errors can include <u>spatial errors</u> (e.g., for the *salute*, the hand touches the cheek instead of the forehead), or <u>movement errors</u> (e.g., for *hitch-hiking*, the hand gesture is correct but with wrist rotation instead of forearm oscillation).
Give 2 points for a correct and accurate gesture.

✎ *Use the same procedure as before but say:*
"I will give you the name of an object and ask you to <u>pretend that you have the object in your hand</u>. I will then ask you to show me how to use it. For example, if you have to show how you would use a toothbrush, you could make a gesture like this *(show gesture)*. **Now, how would you use ...?"**
- Show and read aloud the name of each item, one at a time.

🕐 *- Allow a MAXIMUM of 15 sec. per item.*

TRANSITIVE	Scoring**			Comments
1. A glass, pretending it is in your hand	❑ 2 points	❑ 1 point	❑ 0 point	
2. A salt cellar, pretending it is in your hand*	❑ 2 points	❑ 1 point	❑ 0 point	
3. A hammer, pretending it is in your hand	❑ 2 points	❑ 1 point	❑ 0 point	
Total score:		**/6**		

* For the salt cellar, if the examinee pantomimes the use of a salt spoon rather than a pot, ask him/her to show the alternative gesture for a pot.
** Give 0 points for (1) no response after 15 sec. or (2) an unrecognisable gesture (e.g., for hammer, waving hand) or (3) a perseveration from the previous gesture.
Give 1 point for a recognisable but inaccurate gesture, with errors including <u>spatial errors</u> (e.g., for the *glass*, a pouring gesture is made towards the chest instead of the mouth; or in the case of the *glass* and the *salt cellar*, no space is allowed for the object in the hand – note that if no space is allowed for the *hammer*, this should not be considered as error), or <u>incorrect grip</u> errors (e.g., for the *hammer*, the grip indicates that the hammer is being held perpendicular to forearm), or <u>movement errors</u> (e.g., for the *hammer*, the oscillation is too small to be effective for a hammer or for the *salt cellar*, a big throwing movement rather than a shaking movement is made), or an <u>incomplete sequence of action</u> (e.g., for the *salt cellar*, the grip is correct but there is no shaking of the pot), or <u>concretisation</u>, i.e., the use of an irrelevant object or body part (e.g., holding the other hand, or a pen for the *hammer/glass* or the *salt cellar*).
Give 2 points for each correct and accurate gesture.

Condition of testing (1=normal; NT or stopped due to 2=aphasia; 3=visual/spatial; 4=confusion; 5=fatigue; 6=motor; 7=other.....)	_____
Hand used	❑ left ❑ right
Total score (summing scores for transitive and intransitive gestures)	_____ /12

15. GESTURE RECOGNITION

📄   *Test Book pp. 101–112.*

✏️   ***"I am going to produce a gesture, I would like you to choose a meaning that matches my gesture. For example, if I show you this gesture"*** *(show the gesture for 'be quiet' and repeat the gesture while showing and reading the multiple choice possibilities),* ***"and give you these meanings: counting, be quiet, hello, it's crazy; 'be quiet' is the meaning that best matches the gesture. Now if I show you this gesture, what does it mean?"***
      - Always repeat the gesture while showing and reading aloud the multiple choice possibilities.

🕐   *- MAXIMUM 15 sec. per item.*

INTRANSITIVE

Show gesture of	Response			
1. (Come over) ✋ moving the hand towards you	❑ **Come over**	❑ Salute	❑ Go away	❑ No
2. (Good) 👍	❑ Hitch-hiking	❑ Applause	❑ I swear	❑ **Good**
3. (Goodbye) ✋ moving the hand from the left to the right	❑ Stop	❑ **Goodbye**	❑ OK	❑ Thank you

Total score: **/3**

✏️   *Use the same procedure but say:*
      "I am going to pantomime the use of an object; I would like you to choose the object that I am pretending to use. For example, if I show you this gesture" *(show the gesture for toothbrush and repeat the gesture while showing and reading the multiple choice)* ***"and give you these objects: dental floss, shaver, toothbrush, cheese grater; toothbrush is the correct answer. Now if I show you this gesture, which object do I pretend to use?"***
      - Always repeat the gesture while showing and reading aloud the multiple choice possibilities.

🕐   *- Allow a MAXIMUM of 15 sec. per item.*

TRANSITIVE

Show gesture of	Response			
1. cup	❑ teapot	❑ glass	❑ **cup**	❑ perfume
2. key	❑ **key**	❑ tap	❑ doorbell	❑ door handle
3. lighter	❑ gun	❑ match	❑ torch	❑ **lighter**

Total score: **/3**

(1=normal; NT or stopped due to 2=aphasia; 3=visual/spatial; 4=confusion; 5=fatigue; 6=motor; 7=other.....)	_____
Total score (summing scores for transitive and intransitive gestures)	_____ /6

16A. MEANINGLESS GESTURE IMITATION: FOR EXAMINEES USING THEIR RIGHT HAND

🖉   - *Place yourself in front of the examinee.*
      "I am going to carry out some actions, they do not mean anything, but try your best to copy me. I will use this hand" *(use your left hand)* **"and you should mirror what I do with this hand"** *(touch the examinee's right hand).* **"For example, if I lift this hand"** *(lift your hand),* **"you should lift this hand"** *(touch the examinee's hand).* **"Watch carefully how I position my hand, then copy what I do. Wait until I have finished before you start. This is the sequence."** *Hold each gesture in the sequence for 2 sec., then say "now it's your turn."*
      - *Make sure the examinee starts the gesture only when you have finished demonstrating (and not before).*
      - *If the examinee's gesture is incorrect or imprecise, repeat the demonstration (but repeat only ONCE).*

🕐   - *Allow a MAXIMUM of 15 sec. per item.*

Important! Use your LEFT hand to demonstrate the gesture. The examinee should use his/her RIGHT hand.

HAND	Scoring	Comments
1.	❑ 3 points (correct and precise after one presentation) ❑ 2 points (correct and precise after 2nd presentation) ❑ 1 point (only ONE error after 2nd presentation – see below for list of errors*) ❑ 0 point (more than one error, no response or perseveration from a previous item after the 2nd presentation)	
2.	❑ 3 points (correct and precise after 1 presentation) ❑ 2 points (correct and precise after 2nd presentation) ❑ 1 point (only ONE error after 2nd presentation – see below for list of errors*) ❑ 0 point (more than one error, no response or perseveration from a previous item after the 2nd presentation)	
Total score:	**/6**	

* Give 1 point if ONLY ONE of the following errors is committed (during the second attempt):
- incorrect finger/hand position
- incorrect spatial relationship between hand and head
- incomplete movement sequence

✎ *"Now watch carefully how I position my fingers, then copy what I do. Wait until I have finished before you copy. This is the gesture..."* Show each gesture for 2 sec., then say *"now it's your turn."*
- *Make sure the examinee starts the gesture only when you have finished demonstrating (and not before).*
- *If the examinee's gesture is incorrect or imprecise, repeat the demonstration (but repeat only ONCE).*

🕐 - *Allow a MAXIMUM of 15 sec. per item.*

Important! Use your LEFT hand to demonstrate the gesture. The examinee should use his/her RIGHT hand.

FINGER	Scoring*	Comments
1.	❏ 3 points (correct and precise after one presentation) ❏ 2 points (correct and precise after 2nd presentation) ❏ 1 point (only ONE error after 2nd presentation – see below for list of errors*) ❏ 0 point (more than one error, no response or perseveration from a previous item after 2nd presentation)	
2.	❏ 3 points (correct and precise after one presentation) ❏ 2 points (correct and precise after 2nd presentation) ❏ 1 point (only ONE error after 2nd presentation – see below for list of errors*) ❏ 0 point (more than one error, no response or perseveration from a previous item after 2nd presentation)	
Total score:	/6	

* Give 1 point if the following error ONLY is committed (during the second attempt):
  - finger posture is correct but hand orientation is incorrect

Condition of testing (1=normal; NT or stopped due to 2=aphasia; 3=visual/spatial; 4=confusion; 5=fatigue; 6=motor; 7=other.....)	_____
Hand used	❏ left ❏ right
Total score (summing scores for hand and finger posture imitation)	_____/12

16B. MEANINGLESS GESTURE IMITATION: FOR EXAMINEES USING THEIR LEFT HAND

✎   - *Place yourself in front of the examinee.*
     "I am going to carry out some actions, they do not mean anything, but try your best to copy me. I will use this hand" *(use your right hand)* ***"and you should mirror what I do with this hand*** *(touch the examinee's left hand).* ***"For example, if I lift this hand"*** *(lift your hand),* ***"you should lift this hand"*** *(touch the examinee's hand).* ***"Watch carefully how I position my hand, then copy what I do. Wait until I have finished before you start. This is the sequence..."***   *Hold each gesture in the sequence for 2 sec., then say* ***"now it's your turn."***
     - *Make sure the examinee starts the gesture only when you have finished demonstrating (and not before).*
     - *If the examinee's gesture is incorrect or imprecise, repeat the demonstration (but repeat only ONCE).*

🕐   - *Allow a MAXIMUM of 15 sec. per item.*

Important! Use your RIGHT hand to demonstrate the gesture. The examinee should use his/her LEFT hand.

HAND	Scoring	Comments
1.	❏ 3 points (correct and precise after one presentation) ❏ 2 points (correct and precise after 2nd presentation) ❏ 1 point (only ONE error after 2nd presentation – see below for list of errors*) ❏ 0 point (more than one error, no response or perseveration from a previous item after 2nd presentation)	
2.	❏ 3 points (correct and precise after one presentation) ❏ 2 points (correct and precise after 2nd presentation) ❏ 1 point (only ONE error after 2nd presentation – see below for list of errors*) ❏ 0 point (more than one error, no response or perseveration from a previous item after 2nd presentation)	
Total score:	**/6**	

* Give 1 point if ONLY ONE of the following errors is committed (during the second attempt):
     - incorrect finger/hand position
     - incorrect spatial relationship between hand and head
     - incomplete movement sequence

> ✎ **"Now watch carefully how I position my fingers, then copy what I do. Wait until I have finished before you copy. This is the gesture..."** *Show the gesture for 2 sec., then say* **"now it's your turn".**
> - *Make sure the examinee starts the gesture only when you have finished demonstrating (and not before).*
> - *If the examinee's gesture is incorrect or imprecise, repeat the demonstration (but repeat only ONCE).*
> ⏲ - *Allow a MAXIMUM of 15 sec. per item.*

Important! Use your RIGHT hand to demonstrate the gesture. The examinee should use his/her LEFT hand.

FINGER	Scoring*	Comments
1.	❑ 3 points (correct and precise after one presentation) ❑ 2 points (correct and precise after 2nd presentation) ❑ 1 point (only ONE error after 2nd presentation – see below for list of errors*) ❑ 0 point (more than one error, no response or perseveration from a previous item after 2nd presentation)	
2.	❑ 3 points (correct and precise after one presentation) ❑ 2 points (correct and precise after 2nd presentation) ❑ 1 point (only ONE error after 2nd presentation – see below for list of errors*) ❑ 0 point (more than one error, no response or perseveration from a previous item after 2nd presentation)	

	Total score:	/6

* Give 1 point if the following error ONLY is committed (during the second attempt):
   - finger posture is correct but hand orientation is incorrect

Condition of testing (1=normal; NT or stopped due to 2=aphasia; 3=visual/spatial; 4=confusion; 5=fatigue; 6=motor; 7=other.....)	_____
Hand used	❑ left ❑ right
Total score (summing scores for hand and finger posture imitation)	_____/12

17. TASK RECALL – DELAYED RECOGNITION

📄   *Test Book pp. 113–122.*

✎   **"Here are some questions about the tasks we have done today."**
      - *Show AND read aloud each question and the accompanying multiple choice possibilities.*

🕐   - *Allow a MAXIMUM of 15 sec. per item.*

Recognition	Multiple choice	Comments
1. "Which item did I present to you?"	❑ **1** ❑ 2 ❑ 3 ❑ 4	
2. "What did you have to read?"	❑ 1 ❑ 2 ❑ **3** ❑ 4	
3. "What did you have to remember?"	❑ 1 ❑ **2** ❑ 3 ❑ 4	
4. "Which item did you have to name?"	❑ 1 ❑ **2** ❑ 3 ❑ 4	
5. What did I ask you to do? **MIME THE ACTIONS** while reading the multiple choice possibilities: For (1) move 1 hand with 1 finger raised horizontally (✋ →) For (2) raise 2 fingers on a hand (✌) For (3) snap your fingers with one hand For (4) put your hands in the same position as in the visual extinction task	❑ 1 ❑ 2 ❑ 3 ❑ **4**	
6. "What did I play to you from a recording?"	❑ **1** ❑ 2 ❑ 3 ❑ 4	
7. "Which item did you have to cross out?"	❑ 1 ❑ 2 ❑ 3 ❑ **4**	
8. "Which object did I ask you to use?"	❑ 1 ❑ 2 ❑ **3** ❑ 4	
9. "For which picture did you have to make a sentence?"	❑ 1 ❑ **2** ❑ 3 ❑ 4	
10. "Which gesture did I ask you to do?"	❑ 1 ❑ 2 ❑ 3 ❑ **4**	

Condition of testing (1=normal; NT or stopped due to 2=aphasia; 3=visual/spatial; 4=confusion; 5=fatigue; 6=motor; 7=other.....)	_____
Total score (if all tests were presented to the examinee) NOTE: If not all 10 tasks were presented, write NA in the box here.	_____/10
Modified total score (if some tests were NOT presented to the examinee) NOTE: If all 10 tasks were presented, write NA in the box here.	_____/_____

18. WORD/NONWORD WRITING

📄   *Examinee's booklet.*

✎   **"I will read you some words. Please try to write each word down."**

🕐   - *STOP if NO-RESPONSE is made to the first 3 words and skip the nonword writing.*

WORDS	Response
1. mustard	
2. scissors	
3. thinking	
4. although	

✎   **"I will now give you a nonword, that is, a word that does not exist, and again please write it down."**

NONWORD	
5. troom (with **oom** like in *room*)	

NOTE: Only the following spellings for the nonword are acceptable: troom, trume, treum.

Condition of testing (1=normal; NT or stopped due to 2=aphasia; 3=visual/spatial; 4=confusion; 5=fatigue; 6=motor; 7=other.....)	_____
Number of correct responses NOTE: If stopped because of no-response to the first 3 words, score=0/5.	_____/5

19. NUMBER/PRICE/TIME READING

📄   *Test Book pp. 123–125.*

✎   **"I will show you some written numbers, prices and clock times. Please can you read them."**
- *If the examinee read 539 as "5-3-9" instead of the correct response "five hundred and thirty nine", say* **"Can you read it like a whole number, as if you are describing the number of people in a room?"**

🕐   - *Allow a MAXIMUM of 15 sec. per number.*
- *STOP if NO-RESPONSE is made to the first 3 numbers.*

NUMBERS	Response
1. 539	
2. 2,304	
3. 17,290	

Score (correct responses):   /3

✎   **"Now I will show you prices. Please can you read them."**
- *If the examinee does not say "pounds" on the first item say* **"Can you please read this price again and make clear that it is a price?"**

PRICE	Response
1. £3.99	
2. £109.50	
3. £724.89	

Score (correct responses):   /3

✎   **"Now I will show you some clock times. Please can you read them."**

TIME*	Response
1. 9:30	
2. 2:45	
3. 6:10	

Score (correct responses):   /3

* Absolute and relative clock reading is accepted (e.g., *nine thirty* and *half past nine*)

Condition of testing (1=normal; NT or stopped due to 2=aphasia; 3=visual/spatial; 4=confusion; 5=fatigue; 6=motor; 7=other.....)	_____
Total number of correct responses NOTE: If stopped because of no-response to the first 3 numbers, score=0/9.	_____ /9

---

20. NUMBER WRITING

📄   *Examinee's Booklet.*

✎   **"I will read some numbers. Please write down the numbers as indicated."** *Numbers should be systematically repeated once while the examinee is writing.*

🕐   - *MAXIMUM 15 sec. per number.*
- *STOP if NO-RESPONSE on both of the first 2 numbers.*

NUMBER	Response
1. 807	
2. 12,500	

✎   **"Now I will read some prices; please write down the prices as indicated."**
- *If the examinee does not write "£" on the first item say* **"Can you please write this price again and make clear that it is a price?"**

PRICE	
3. £5.99	
4. £25.50	
5. £329.89	

Condition of testing (1=normal; NT or stopped due to 2=aphasia; 3=visual/spatial; 4=confusion; 5=fatigue; 6=motor; 7=other.....)	_____
Total number of correct responses NOTE: If stopped because of no-response on first 2 numbers, score=0/5.	_____ /5

21. CALCULATION

📄   *Test Book pp. 126–129 and Examinee's Booklet.*

✏️   **"I will ask you to do some calculations. You can use this page if you want to write the calculation or write the response"** *(give the relevant page from the Examinee's Booklet).* **"How much is..."**
    - *Show and read each calculation aloud.*

🕐   - *Allow a MAXIMUM of 30 sec. per item.*

👄   - *In the case of an unreliable verbal production, ask the examinee to write down their answers.*

	Response
1. $15 + 38 = (53)$	
2. $45 - 7 = (38)$	
3. $8 \times 6 = (48)$	
4. $63 \div 7 = (9)$	

Total score (correct responses): [/4]

Specify if the response is written rather than given orally: _____

Condition of testing	_____
(1=normal; NT or stopped due to 2=aphasia; 3=visual/spatial; 4=confusion; 5=fatigue; 6=motor; 7=other.....)	
Modality of response	❑ oral
	❑ written
Number of correct responses	_____/4

22. COMPLEX FIGURE COPY

📄   *Examinee's Booklet, stopwatch. See Appendices 4 and 5 of the Manual for details on scoring.*

✏️   - *Hide the figure while giving the instructions.*
    "I will show you a figure. Please copy it as best you can."
    - *Show the figure to the examinee and record the time.*

🕐   - *Allow a MAXIMUM of 5 min.*

		Scoring	
1. Middle square	presence	❑ yes	❑ no
	shape/proportion	❑ correct	❑ incorrect
2. Middle arrow	presence	❑ yes	❑ no
	shape/proportion	❑ correct	❑ incorrect
	placement	❑ correct	❑ incorrect
3. Middle right curve	presence	❑ yes	❑ no
	shape/proportion	❑ correct	❑ incorrect
	placement	❑ correct	❑ incorrect
4. Middle left curve	presence	❑ yes	❑ no
	shape/proportion	❑ correct	❑ incorrect
	placement	❑ correct	❑ incorrect
5. Middle cross	presence	❑ yes	❑ no
	shape/proportion	❑ correct	❑ incorrect
	placement	❑ correct	❑ incorrect
6. Middle main diagonal	presence	❑ yes	❑ no
	shape/proportion	❑ correct	❑ incorrect
	placement	❑ correct	❑ incorrect
7. Left diagonal end (3 bars)	presence	❑ yes	❑ no
	shape/proportion	❑ correct	❑ incorrect
	placement	❑ correct	❑ incorrect
8. Left rectangle	presence	❑ yes	❑ no
	shape/proportion	❑ correct	❑ incorrect
	placement	❑ correct	❑ incorrect
9. Left horizontal bar	presence	❑ yes	❑ no
	shape/proportion	❑ correct	❑ incorrect
	placement	❑ correct	❑ incorrect
10. Left double oblique bars (parallel)	presence	❑ yes	❑ no
	shape/proportion	❑ correct	❑ incorrect
	placement	❑ correct	❑ incorrect
11. Left circle	presence	❑ yes	❑ no
	shape/proportion	❑ correct	❑ incorrect
	placement	❑ correct	❑ incorrect

12. Right diagonal end (1 curved line)	presence	❏ yes	❏ no
	shape/proportion	❏ correct	❏ incorrect
	placement	❏ correct	❏ incorrect
13. Right rectangle	presence	❏ yes	❏ no
	shape/proportion	❏ correct	❏ incorrect
	placement	❏ correct	❏ incorrect
14. Right horizontal bar	presence	❏ yes	❏ no
	shape/proportion	❏ correct	❏ incorrect
	placement	❏ correct	❏ incorrect
15. Right double oblique (triangle shape)	presence	❏ yes	❏ no
	shape/proportion	❏ correct	❏ incorrect
	placement	❏ correct	❏ incorrect
16. Right double dot	presence	❏ yes	❏ no
	shape/proportion	❏ correct	❏ incorrect
	placement	❏ correct	❏ incorrect

Note: When scoring an erroneous production, try not to penalise the same error twice.

Condition of testing (1=normal; NT or stopped due to 2=aphasia; 3=visual/spatial; 4=confusion; 5=fatigue; 6=motor; 7=other.....)	_____
Total score (1 point for each "yes" or "correct" box)	_____ /47
Total MIDDLE score ONLY	_____ /17
Total LEFT score ONLY	_____ /15
Total RIGHT score ONLY	_____ /15

Please tick any of the following if they are evident in the examinee's figure copy:

❏ Closing-in Behaviour (the copy is made very close to or on top of the original figure)
❏ Micrographia (the copy is less than half the size of the original figure, <u>both</u> in height and width)
❏ Macrographia (the copy is more than one and a half times the size of the original figure, <u>both</u> in height and width)
❏ Neglect (the performance is substantially worse on the left <u>or</u> right parts relative to the other parts of the figure)
❏ Additions/Perseverations (the drawing contains elements not present in the original figure)

23. INSTRUCTION COMPREHENSION

🖉 *Evaluate the examinee's overall understanding of the instructions*

Condition of testing (1=normal; NT or stopped due to 2=aphasia; 3=visual/spatial; 4=confusion; 5=fatigue; 6=motor; 7=other.....)	_____
Total score (1=poor understanding even after repetition, 2=relatively good understanding but instructions need often to be repeated, 3=good understanding, almost no need to repeat the instructions) NOTE: This assessment should be *primarily* based on the scoring for instruction/question comprehension in the following tasks: orientation (1a–1b–1c), sentence construction (3), rule finding and concept switching (10) and auditory attention (11).	

BCoS

ISBN 978-1-84872-099-2 [Test pack, including the Manual]
ISBN 978-1-84872-107-4 [Examiner's Booklet]
ISBN 978-1-84872-110-4 [Examiner's Booklet B]

Errata

Examiner's Booklet and Examiner's Booklet B:

p. 3, task 2, instruction line 4, replace "*...any of the 4 first pictures*" with "*...all of the 4 first pictures*".

p. 4, first line of instruction: "*See Appendix 4 of the Manual ...*" should read "*See Appendix 3 of the Manual ...*".

p. 11, practice 1 box, the horizontal line below the line "3. Goodbye" should not be bold.

p. 17, task 16A, second hand sequence, first position photo should show right hand action, not left hand.

p. 21, task 18, the bold horizontal line below line "3. Thinking" is missing.

p.22, task 19, the bold horizontal line below line "3. 17,290" is missing.

p.22, task 20, the bold horizontal line below line "2. 12,500" is missing.

Manual:

p. 23, "Apple Cancellation – total": In the "≤64" group, the cut off score should be "42", not "2".